IKTSUARPOK

Nora Nadjarian is a poet and short fiction writer from Cyprus. In 2020, she represented Cyprus in the Hay Festival's *Europa 28*: *Visions for the Future*. Her work has been included in various anthologies and publications around the world. She has won or been commended in numerous international competitions, including the Mslexia Poetry Competition (2021).

ISBN: 978-1-915760-54-8

Cover designed by Aaron Kent

Edited By Charlie Baylis

Typeset by Aaron Kent

Broken Sleep Books Ltd
Rhydwen
Talgarreg
Ceredigion
SA44 4HB

Broken Sleep Books Ltd
Fair View
St Georges Road
Cornwall
PL26 7YH

Iktsuarpok

Nora Nadjarian

Broken Sleep Books

For my father

Contents

I tipped all my words overboard

Iktsuarpok	11
The Last Polar Bear Spoke Yiddish	12
Frozen House	13
The Unbearable	14
Ferocious	15
Acts of Tenderness	16
Downpour	17
The coast guard found an empty life raft	18
Hammam	19
For a moment I forget that the river is complicated	20
Jonquil	21
Memoirs of a Beautiful Daughter	22
You Tread on my Dreams	23
Black Sheep	24
Bedside	25
In the Land of Drought	26
Murmuration	27

I'm alone in this poem and trying to make sense of it

The Egg was Blue	31
What you were looking for, have you found it?	32
Dusk	33
How it Begins and Ends	34
In the News of the World	35
At Twenty Minutes to Nine	36
The Seagull	37
Rooster	38
Emily, I never wrote a poem about butterflies	39
ETD	40
We didn't die, we levitated	41
Tattooed onto my Memory	42
I have made a note of –	43
About a boy who is pure of heart	44
Thirteen Ways of Looking at Uncertainty	45

Our voices were stupid anyway, so we stopped screaming

Ghost Mountain   49

Noah's Ark   50

The Untranslatability of Silence   51

Although   52

Carousel   53

The Perfect Child Emerges   54

Clay Animation   55

No Answers   56

Almost a Poem about War   57

Everything else is Nothing   58

I'm doing my best to breathe

Smaragdine   61

Labyrinth   62

After Breakup #7   63

Nothin' but a pain in your heart   64

Translation of a Misunderstanding   65

Undoing my Hex   66

Uninhibited in Another Language   67

Hibiscus   68

The Singular of Paparazzi   69

The Salesgirl says the Mannequin is Not for Sale 70

Millennium Bug   71

In which the Doctor speaks Gibberish   72

The Great Wave   73

Feet in the Bowl   74

Acknowledgements   77

I tipped all my words overboard

Iktsuarpok

An Inuit word, meaning the impatient excitement for a visit that makes you look out the window countless times in the hope of seeing your guest arrive.

I found a word and I'm riding a wild white woah.
No, I found a word which is a window, and there's snow
outside. I found this word for you and because I'm waiting
and because sometimes the hour takes too long. I found this
word without warning, for warmth, but you will not be late, I know.
I found a special word for the naked hooves galloping on the carpet and,
somewhere else, life is orderly. No, it is rare to find a word I can't even say
out loud, that describes how this room feels right now. I found the word which
starts here and ends when you arrive. I found a word which exists because you do.
There is another word for waiting and this o'clock strikes as your feet sink in soft snow
and the door opens, your smile a blizzard. I want to kiss the surprising mouth in your hello.

The Last Polar Bear Spoke Yiddish

He can tell you the word for white.
Vays, and his wise eyes turn
fierce. He slits his words in half
like fish. The things he has seen!
Oh, little ultra-violet world,
he's forgotten how not to speak
of entrails, of punctured guts.
The last polar bear shivers,
barely remembers food, blubber,
comfort. The reporter asks him
to comment on the future of ice.
Slush puppies, he says, the cracks
around him gaping. At night, sleep
is a curious trick. His dead wife sings:
Vays vi milek, vays vi shney.
White as milk, white as snow.

Frozen House

All the robins turned white, even their lashes (if they have lashes). There is no border between white and white. Will we talk again once our voices have thawed? How cold I am in this bed and all the heating on. In that scene in Doctor Zhivago, she hates him for entering the frozen house. There's a candelabra she can't face because the flame is dead. *Where will I go?* she wonders. *Where will I magically disappear to?* Yesterday, my feet crunched all the way from the forest, today they will crunch all the way back. The bear's breath is warm, its voice large. It says *Did you say goodbye to love? Keep your coat on a little longer.*

The Unbearable

A pyromaniac turns up the volume and sets the grass on fire. An über-summer, unbridled and hellishly hot. I want to write a poem about burying myself in a bathtub of blue ice cubes, about how August is a killjoy and the sun ungodly. The barking of the dogs hurts my ears, they want, they pant. At least it's temporary, this damnation, a border between one season and the next. All the time I think, selfishly, my skin, my skin, sticky sugar. My mouth is thirst. The whirr of a fan sends me to sleep. In the dream you say *The world is disastrous but bearable*. You bring me lemon granita which tastes of mirage.

Ferocious

Fish are dropped from a plane into the greedy river. They are small slivers of bigger fish, falling in slow-motion. There's fish pandemonium in complete silence and the water is murky, crocodile-friendly. Fertilizer dumped into the river, says my father, everything hush-hush, and I wake up bitten by piranha teeth. I check my body for completeness, for all the parts I know. My breasts, my arms, my belly, I'm all here but there's a bright colour between my legs. I will have eggs, and children, add to the population of 7.9 billion. The red-bellied piranha is on the news, opening and closing his mouth, chewing human flesh. My mother says there are fish which look like stones covered with warts. They blend in exactly, then spit venom when stepped on. They're waiting, cracking shells. The river we're all swimming in is different shades of blood.

Acts of Tenderness

The moon, a huge mint in the sky. We licked the pictures in the story book, marzipan house and dark crepe paper. A witch fed cats with leftover mouse tails. A witch offered us cupcakes with lemony white icing. We said, 'No, no, thank you,' politely. She insisted and her voice was incense. Her voice was sweet smoke. In her garden was a skilful fox, a scavenger that stole, cracked eggs and fed its cubs. An urgent animal, smooth and articulate. The house was full of possibilities; it waited for us like a gift, its door ajar. We eventually gave in, said 'Yes, yes, please,' bit into the sweet walls, buried our tongues in the soft whipped cream of the floor, our faces scented with rosewater and syrup. Hansel said, 'Who do you think we are now?' I said, 'Who we were before,' but I knew that was the wrong answer, and the witch laughed. We were curled by her side while she dragged on the hookah. 'Live lush stories you'll never forget. I'll sell your kidneys and liver,' she said, stroked our heads. 'There are people who need them. You have such luminous hair, Gretel. You should keep it long.'

Downpour

From afar it looks like nothing but it hits us obliquely and hard and turns us into shivering puppets. It pelts down on our heads and thoughts, the sky slashed and gushing. You say you're sorry and I ask *About what?* You say you're sorry about the rain, how mercilessly it falls. There's a gun in someone's hand and you keep saying you're sorry, I say *It's not your fault,* all this shattering is just a storm but we need to find our faces, all the world is blind. Still thrashing against us, this rain, as if we were rocks. Still killing us, this rain, with its bullets.

The coast guard found an empty life raft

We were heading to Bermuda, hit something large on the way.

Might have been a statue of God. Or a whale.

Delgado said I think we've found something, I don't know what.

We examined the emptiness of the fish net.

Details: the salty eye of the beholder, the quirky quotation marks

when no one spoke, the name of the silver-purple-yellow fish, *Pirate*.

The coastline called us back.

Throw out everything you own, lose weight.

I tipped all my words overboard.

Lastly, the unreliable narrator.

Hammam

*After **The Turkish Bath**, Jean-Auguste-Dominique Ingres*

One woman says there is nothing prudish about our bodies. We all agree that our curves look brave in the steam, our hips spilling out into the headiness. Our sweat in big, round drops beneath our breasts, in rivulets down our bellies, between our legs. The tiles are blue and gold, the floor slippery. A whole-body scrub with the *kese* mitt by a girl who douses us, then massages our boldness with something like hatred in her hands. Later we lie on the scalding octagon of marble, flat on our backs. Courtesans, they call us, we're used to this position. The soaring dome above us has a ceiling of stars cut out as skylights. Our tongues sizzle with the sherbet of life. Next door, a tap drips in the silence of his bathroom. A voyeur, his easel and paints.

For a moment I forget that the river is complicated

The sodden grey-dull sky is reflected, and some ducks. An art teacher once taught me dirty colours. The river is smelly with this swelling silence, and a couple walk past, hand in hand, unsuspecting of what happens when filth breaks its banks. The solitary swan glides, satisfied and maddeningly mute. I marvel at its indifference and whiteness. Mostly its indifference, compared to how strangely and bitterly I sometimes cry in public.

Jonquil

The jonquil speaks in yellow. As for him, his body lies on the grass and how different the days are now, light crushing the sky, his body crushing the green. The jonquil says dreams are memories steeped in syrup. He's still licking a drop off his lips as he wakes up, sunned and content. The jonquil reminds him that the past is another colour. He still has a memory to prove they existed, one blank afternoon in Edinburgh. The jonquil says lemonade for the parched and his confused tongue agrees. She was brighter than anything he remembers.

Memoirs of a Beautiful Daughter

After Simone de Beauvoir

In Paris, in museums, a wilderness of spaces. The day would come, I repeated. Dancing, singing and dressing-up in my diary, it exasperated me, I was still nobody. The pursuit of truths, distress in glowing colours and Love was impossible. A song of the cuckoo, without being able to explain. Failed in several attempts to make friends. Walks in the Luxembourg Gardens: pistachio green, strawberry red, pastel lilac. To tell the truth, the more difficult a life, when you want beauty. Fits of bad temper, isolation, the world in chaos. Not long after that, the self that others saw. I discovered that hope was millions of hearts and lights. This great fire was blazing in me. Am I beautiful? Am I beautiful? I asked him, my mouth dreamed. He lost his answers but I saw him again. Looked me up and down, masked the abyss completely. A little further on –bars, laughter, sex. With some embarrassment, I wanted to unhammer my heart. Just one kiss, but perhaps that was pride, and not love? A fixation on many months later, this great change when I was, finally, somebody. A kiss was not his mouth, but the world.

You Tread on my Dreams

But I, being poor, have only my dreams; / I have spread my dreams under your feet...
— W. B. Yeats

I could tell you so much about what happened but,
really, there is just showing not telling in our house and, yes, I
write and sweat a thousand fragments and long lines, being
the poet of the family who collects words like *impecunious*, poor
poet of the family, and *qu'est-ce que tu as,* what do you have
they ask in French when they mean *what's wrong.* If only
I could make sense of what happened. In my
journal I have written: I don't want to have bad dreams.

It keeps coming back like a starving wolf and I
know he's dead but I run away, write about what I have
seen catching up on me and treading on my thoughts spread
out on the floor like printed sheets in disorder and my
cauchemar sounds worse than nightmares or bad dreams.
There is a film unsuitable for girls wearing pink, girls under-
15. Lo-lee-ta and all the filth and tangle of the French in your
lies and a tongue-twister tying my little feet.

Black Sheep

On the doorstep the night is quiet, so is the sheep. *I never thought* – is all my mother can utter. *You must be hungry, you must be tired, and where have you been?* You know how your stomach turns into knots? I try to think of something bright, like marmalade, but the knot gets tighter. *I've been waiting for this*, says my father, livid. My mother's voice soft, but useless, my brother alive, but a sheep. There's something defeated in the way he looks at us. How he stands at the door, neither coming in, nor leaving, neither crying, nor laughing, the way he always was, at the edge of something.

Bedside

Finally, your son says *Forgive me*. It sounds like a prompt for canned laughter but your daughter is closer, moving and not moving, cracking her knuckles with remembrance. Your wife, holes in her eyes, white flowers on her dress, will stand here forever and long after you've gone, begging you not to do it. The crushed fruit, syrupy-red, is your heart. Is your heart.

In the Land of Drought

I cared for you in the wilderness, / In the land of drought.

— Hosea 13:5

i

A woman held a clay pot   couldn't water her plant

A man carried two bags of rain   saving it for dry times

They said on the news   save some   for when God shuts the sky

The parched trees   did not speak   held their tongues

Lips and leaves   together tight   My father

lit an angry cigarette   The tap was on empty

Crows squalled   the way they do

We wanted rain   our tongues white

The sea   swallowed salt   raged and spat

Brand new rain   distilled   is what we hoped for

Let rain   wash our souls   said my mother

It never came   We became wilderness

faces   made of   dust

ii

Glad to lend a hand   I said   to the neighbour

It's alright and it was all alright   carrying the bucket

The gecko smiled   l smiled

We arranged flowers   in empty vases   their stalks drooping

and the dying neighbour said   Those flowers are dead

The evil eye   is evil and blue   and cracked

She read   my face   and her face   fell

No rain? No rain In Turkish   in Greek   we spoke

Birds pecked   and blinded   cherries

iii

The bud   the first joy   of everything

waiting to burst   they said

Murmuration

The chaos is green,
so green, you'd think it was the lodestar
with a neon sign for the end of the world, but NO WAY –
the blue just keeps blooming with birds. A method in this madness,
in this murmuration so bright, you'd think an enormous
old tree decided to lend the sky its leaves.
They tell you there is still time. Don't you dare think otherwise.
The future is a noisy and high-pitched place, thrilling with possibilities.
A great whoosh of them, shiny plumage, iridescent necks.
They insist there IS justice in the world, just listen,
because after the drought and the fire, come wet seasons.
Time is on the move and no matter what, there will always be tide.
The ebb and flow of budgerigars. How to explain this?
This explosion of sound and colour and sparks flying, spiralling, the vane turning
and turning, and good news travelling fast. For once, good news,
mesmerising news, flashing before you in the semaphore
of thousands of wings.

I'm alone in this poem and trying to make sense of it

The Egg was Blue

When my father said it was raining in the living room and he needed an umbrella, we knew. It was raining and he needed an umbrella but he was holding an egg. The egg he was holding was blue, he said, and he was hungry, could he eat it. He was hungry and the egg was tiny and blue. But then God chirped, he said. My father held the egg and there was God inside, he couldn't see but could feel the life in there. He held it close to his heart and it was raining blue inside him, he said. My father's body was an egg-shell, his face cracking slowly, without a word. We knew.

What you were looking for, have you found it?

We stand and wave. No, we stand and wait. We are here and Mother opens her purse and flips a coin, heads he dies, tails he dies. You lie very still, your mouth half open, dreaming of the colour of lemons. How can you sleep through all this, three minutes past eleven, sleep ad nauseum, sleep ad infinitum? The Eureka variety is the brightest, you used to say, the word tart on your tongue. There's this thing called a hand, for touching – but I daren't. I daren't use the tips of my fingers to ask. The bulb flickers, dims. Your ribs are cracked open, life leaking out. The rain will carry on without you.

Dusk

There's something about troubled sentences wrung out of us or
How one day certainty abandons us or
How we grow old and regret or
How we forget or
How
The owl knows all the answers. Yesterday we had a conversation a very long time ago.
It was all in sepia, like the dead.

How it Begins and Ends

It begins like this. You walk along the line and you're still on the line two months later. You want to get off and be a part of the whole structure, like sunflowers which fit into the earth, shoulder to shoulder, head to head. You feel the need to open your front door, to let everyone in.

There was this face on TV, luminous, it was God reading the nine o'clock news. He was saying tomorrow will be a miracle, tomorrow will be a burden lifting itself, tomorrow will surprise us with the way this story ends.

It ends like this. You walk along the line and you're still on the line two months later. You watch the nine o'clock news every night at nine o'clock.

In the News of the World

After Riffat Abbas

In the news of the world
Find God and good and lovers, my friend.

Even if they tell us nothing
Even if they tell us everything
We can write our own *surprise!* version, my friend.

Even if peace is war and truth is fake
Even if kindness is exhausted
Let us consider a bulletin of hope, my friend.

La La Land has stolen the show
The pandemic is on the floor
Let us break unbelievable stories, my friend.

At Twenty Minutes to Nine

The old vinyl record is scratching itself to death and the city so far away. She says she was once in love and now it's just walls. The world is something of a beauty, something of a beast, and Miss H. wants to stop the game. Every now and then we are fools, she says, the sun hides and seeks. On the comb in her lap some white hairs, ivory threads. Memories are rotten déjà vu and what-was, served on a polished tray. All night long the wedding cake is eaten by darkness.

The Seagull

I forgot to tell you that there is betrayal in every play. It is make-believe but you believe each word. The family sits round a table, eats a seagull. Mother: *I don't believe that birds have souls.* Father: *I love the uneven, roasted skin.* Brother: *Remember how brutal its eyes were, when it squawked*? The dinner table is lacquered yellow with a touch of the bird's fury. They tear the seagull apart, as if blaming it for their hunger. Nina says a pale-white prayer and asks: *Have you learnt nothing from that last line?*

Rooster

In our back garden the rooster was brilliant white and had rusty eyes.
I'm sorry about turning the sky on and off, he said.
Another time, he said I'm sorry about 4am.
Once, he just said I'm sorry.
One night the rooster died. His voice strangled,
one dead eye terrifyingly loud.

Emily, I never wrote a poem about butterflies

It was always about a cockroach or a forest of abandoned memories. She says there is no point in staring at a dead light. I say: you and I are so alike, your words devastate me. I write and I read the poems out loud and she listens. I throw her a phrase for the fun of it and she asks what language, and I say I don't know, do you need to know? She says language is a game but a very lovely one. There are no two identical ones, anywhere. In some languages a J is a Y. In some languages a sentence is music. Some languages are dying. Some languages are already ghosts. She tells me to stop writing grief, to take it to the river and drown it. How can I? It's my grief and yours, it's yours too, it's ours. I say to her: think of words we wrote, then drowned, just think, how ugly our hands. We sit and study our hands, these terrible, terrified hands, because we can't look each other in the eye.

ETD

Your estimated time of departure is five o'clock but it could be eleven. You'll lick litmus paper for fun. You'll be force-fed gazpacho, blue raspberry slush. This yapping child is too close, beware its rough tongue. It knows more about you than you know yourself, the way dogs sniff out the mule. I say you, but I mean me. In security they suspect I'm an alias. The poem has leaked onto my passport like sour coffee and *What do these hieroglyphs mean?* the dog snarls. I'm stranded between this and that country. I crumple a fistful of documents, first drafts, love the sound they make. I'm on the run, smuggling words, going home to my hide-out. What if I tell him the poem wrote itself? That I had little to do with it, that I washed my hands of it in the Ladies' toilets? The cleaner mopped around my guilty feet. *What forest is this?* she thought. *What leaves?* but I can't be sure of her thoughts, though the toilets smelled of pine. I'm boarding, and I have an unbearable longing to say to the Hello, Welcome *I'm a great poet.* One day I'll be caught.

We didn't die, we levitated

A howling dog scratching at the door. More howling dogs, scratching. The fiddler trying to make sense of the world, trying. Trying, again. The couple wants to flee, to fly, the couple holds hands and levitates. The sky is red hot with war. The couple levitates, as in a painting. *Remember all those times I said I love you?* he asks but she can't hear him. *Are we still alive?* she asks, but he can't hear her. A door creaks open. People scratching at the sky, *Save us, save us!* The fiddler tries for music, again. Listen. A country is being chainsawed.

Tattooed onto my Memory

This is not really about tattoos, or memory. It's about the rottenness of cliché. I read a poem about nuclear war which had a balloon in it, and an electric toothbrush. In every war, a grand piano with falling teeth. My poems collide. The war burns paper lanterns and gouges a doll's eyes. A bloated belly doll, with plastic arms and legs that melt into the hot sea. An octopus with tentacles braided tight like catastrophes. Chasm in a human brain. The headlines titillate and if you say the word long enough it's WARWARWAR. It's the night before the nuclear war and we're drunk as dogs. I am a limp puppet on the floor, the light bulb is a distant moon. You say there will be war, first one in donkey's years. In the year of the donkey, America presses a button, Russia presses a button, North Korea presses a button, South Korea presses a button, China presses a button. God presses a button. You and I press a button together, like cutting a wedding cake. Then you say your battery needs to be charged and you leave. So now I'm alone in this poem and trying to make sense of it.

I have made a note of —

consciences being schlepped everywhere and that's life, blushing. You said:
Last time I saw you, your father was still alive, your good father. My good father.
As I walked up the hill I thought he'd be there to greet me but instead, there
was this soft breeze, a blistering sky. My last poem was a kind of fury and I
shredded every line. The poet goes on stage and announces *Time is skidding
along, the word-shredding has begun.* We live in times of uncertainty. There
was this grey hum in my thoughts, the opposite of laughter: it was the sound
of listening to nothing at night. But we still write, we write, hold words to the
light. You said: *I have to have something to live for! And a life to live!* Do you
remember back when, two years ago? In my living room, next to the mirror,
a neon green question mark flickers. Two years of locked hope and I-don't-
know-what-to-say, and cycling past myself on a slow journey to nowhere. Day
and night on the Peloton, the poet thinks of a landslide waiting to happen.
Soon, there is a war. On the news, satellite images of *appalling acts,* sometimes
atrocities. The poet makes a note of history and history and history repeating
itself. The poet remembers her father who used to say *This war will end so
badly. It will end so badly, this war, mark my words.* Before and after, we will
be different people.

About a boy who is pure of heart

The answer was yes. Without another word she dropped the moth.
There were messages in a bottle and he was mildly interested.
Tell me a better story, she said. About a boy who is pure of heart.
The idea was to go back to the beginning.

Thirteen Ways of Looking at Uncertainty

After Wallace Stevens

i

It is evening and I don't know
what morning will do
to tomorrow except place bees on its lips.

ii

There is forever and there is never
in a door-slam. Somebody killed our time,
left us behind, between *may* and *be.*

iii

Tend to your garden, Neighbour.
This decay is a kind of beauty.
A barefoot pink rose, petals like sighs.

iv

When did my name crash? And where?
Our mothers are dead with fear, or feared dead.

v

The soldier licking another
soldier's boots from afar, is it possible?
Or it could be a loyal dog.

vi

They will find bones and shoes and
teeth. Eggs they will not understand, crushed
in plastic bags. A haunted Citroën.

vii

And what will become of our hungry breath? We will recite
our alphabet over and over, like a prayer.

viii

I wanted to have a child and now I have
no husband. Today is yesterday, or even last year.

ix

We buried a statue and its voice stared at us through the hole,
said *Keep going.* A bird begged us to pluck her.

x

Mid-sentence, the rain fell.
Our faces shivered when we saw our hands.

xi

Write me a song with no lyrics, if you can.
Make it peaceful, make it a baby.

xii

In the mime scene, at the sight of our demolished house,
we flap our wings. The audience bombards us
with apples and applause.

xiii

We were once human and to human
we may never return.

Our voices were stupid anyway, so we stopped screaming

Ghost Mountain

It all happened a century ago, or more, and we lost a mountain. There is still snow but it is not young. There was a pristine white envelope with a letter for me, from my father, Dearest, explaining that the mountain had gone. We'd lost it to another country. Ditto the Ark and the animals in it. Ditto, Noah. There is no point in crying over melting snow, Dearest. I thought: How can a mountain be lost or won. Impossible! In an old atlas my father showed me ghost countries, ghost mountains. Then he mentioned people. Your mother climbed the mountain in bare feet, she never reached the summit. Snow covered her tracks, we lost her. I wanted to tell you she was adventurous, you're old enough to know. She could have carried you on her back, Dearest, but now it's too late. We only have each other and this illusion of living. Memories are losing their mind, too, caught in a blizzard. I imagine my mother's soul has reached the abandoned Ark. At such altitudes snow becomes hallucination. I will write her a letter. Dearest –

Noah's Ark

In an ark of this size, there will be space enough for us, the out-driven. While we were climbing in, a woman was playing the piano. She was writing a history of drowning souls whose giant confusion became her crescendo. Noah said come in. He was expecting animals in pairs, instead he got the odd humans, the ones who are way out. Come in, he said. This new country, you will live in it, and multiply. The level of water was rising. Look at the water, dark and unclean, like petrol. Suspended in this strange and final place, on top of a frozen mountain, we wrote letters home, dialled numbers, we are alive, we are safe, knowing full well we were not. Noah was a con-man who smiled a lot. He wore a waterproof and carried a torch. And then he switched it off.

The Untranslatability of Silence

My grandfather said his mother lost her voice.
It burnt to ashes one night in Warsaw.
She never spoke again but rang bells,
or whistled, or stitched moments of silence.
Nobody really knew what she was saying –
except the man who had lost his mind
burying bodies, babies, broken stars.

Although

Although we can still talk about it as survivors do
and all the faces in the photos are dead as if the photos have been ripped
or burnt to ashes, collected in envelopes and sealed and sent to lost relatives
there is always the feeling, that gut feeling, that we were never told enough
or that we didn't resist enough or weren't enough, and these people walking
across a desert and sometimes on waves like Jesus, proving that they could,
like he could, cross over borders where people pinpointed them and pointed
at them and couldn't pronounce their long names, even if their lives were
basically the same, except for the drowning, that terrible drowning
the papers wrote about, I know all about it, believe me,
my mouth is ash.

Carousel

The exiles sit on tiny red horses with golden tails and curly manes which
take them exactly nowhere. My small, hunched grandfather asks in twenty
different tongues: When do we arrive? My grandmother, hair in a bun, tuts.
My coquette mother, head going round, tired of circles, asks: When?
I say: I don't know, I'm too young, ask the others. The horses neigh in that
pretty Parisian way carousels turn, and our brains spin until nothing happens,
except that they're all taking photos of us endangered people but we can't stop
the carousel and we can't stop them. Hold on tight, says my father, his face
a nervous gun in a sweaty palm. My sister's screeching and kicking the dead,
red horse: I want to get off! Off! Management says: We're sorry for the trouble.
My grandfather: They're killing us, it's the CIA! His private, repeated headlines.
It's night again and we're still spinning the ghosts, their breath howling in our ears
till we can't hear a thing. Our voices were stupid anyway, so we stopped
screaming. My father's slouched into his body, my mother's hair a strange
garden, the rest of her and us, sullen and hungry and tattered. The horses
are beautifully lacquered. My darlings, when? I don't know, earth's too young
and I don't want to write about death, or dirt, or dusk. Don't want to know
how they, or how we, all turned and turned to dust.

The Perfect Child Emerges

The most beautiful boy, drinking the light. Everything happened fast and there's this story called the future. The child's skin is soft, its body baby-wrinkled and fat with new life. The world says *welcome*, the world says *may your body sleep and wake and sleep, may your eyes blink, your hair and nails grow, and your heart beat, beat, beat.* This child, this mini human, cries and the room fills with the noise of milk and hunger. There will be sucking and sobbing and laughing from the same mouth. Words the colour of tiny turquoise eggs ready to hatch. Shiny new teeth. Then, hair everywhere. Then, with incredible speed away from you, a tall boy runs from one season to the next. Away from this baby in the cot sucking its thumb, oblivious to the sudden earth, the endless sky.

Clay Animation

I like the clay shaping of strangers on the underground
reading papers busy with headlines, books heavy with meaning.
Today it's the penis of the man whose face shines like parquet,
a woman's curved hips making her an urn, the baby's mushroom face
so delightful it could be a tinkle. Shot by shot they seem an extravagance
against the backdrop of blurred faces. They zoom into colour, to summer,
and that is exactly right to my eye. The baby's babbling monologue
provides the soundtrack, as the man slowly smiles at his wife.
She touches her belly, lightly taps that tiny button, a little secret.
A short journey, before doors slide open and they empty into their lives.

No Answers

There is a wisdom in unplugging apparatus during lightning storms.
In the dream there was a shivering redbreast outside the window.
I opened the window and let it in. These hamantaschen are filled
with a celebration of seeds, it said. What are hamantaschen, I asked.
Your seats are L-shaped, a capital L, like love, came the reply.
These objects will keep virtually indefinitely, except in storms,
When poppy seeds fill the air and sesame seeds fall.
There are no answers to everything. Lightning strikes. Unplug.

Almost a Poem about War

After **Triptyque Bleu I, Bleu II, Bleu III**, Joan Miró

I

I'd choose from thousands of incidents this blue tissue and my nosebleed as a beginning. The drops mark the spot and my face does a run, tears of some sort. Or sweat. Meanwhile, hear the bombs next door. Drops of blood gone black on a blue pavement. Rocket fire in the sky destroys with the colour of lipstick. My nosebleed is stupid, like the word *oeuf*, black *egg*, drops of blood. One of the bodies may be that of a child.

II

What if the red scar always shows. In the sky. Twelve houses still stand in the village, minimalistic. The volume of voices decreases, increases, gasps for air. Before that, they'd been swimming in the sea. *Eizeh kef, what fun, walla!* A red match or red snake or a red whatever spoils the scene. Apologies, there was a blue fire, it burned human effort, turned it to rubble, beat the tar out.

III

I will tell you what I know, and it is very little. The sun-kite and black earth face each other, in love or hate. Somebody let go of the string. We may explode. Or not.

Everything else is Nothing

Look at you, with the candlewax hair, melting. Yes, you with the candlewax hair, your hair is dripping down your face and your face is dripping down your chest and there is no more of you. Yes, no more of you, though you believed in God and everything, and everything believed in you. Yes, you rotten apricot, the sun has found the core inside you, everything else is Nothing licking its sticky fingers.

I'm doing my best to breathe

Smaragdine

A surprise to my lobes,
the earrings. Two leaves
suddenly greening
in times of drought.

It was you who explained
green is forgiving,
the way the earth forgets
crimes we commit.

I will write a poem about
the exquisite tint of your kiss,
limey and minty
and smaragdine.

Labyrinth

Plus and minus and the probability that we will never meet again, the impossibility of finding our way to the exit.

Puzzled about the meaning of the enclosure, the eccentricity of the inventor who has us trapped. It's a relationship of sorts.

On a Valentine's card I wrote: Where will I spend eternity? In a maze, with you.

His mind is tattered and he waits for the moment to be brave, to reply. The noise that cicadas make in the heat is a small crime.

When this story's finished, Minotaur, I will burst into tears.

After Breakup #7

Nothing in the bag except a sun-dried tomato. It's here, just one, and what does it mean? *We think you're drying up, it's no use.* What if you take it in your palm (it fits, it sleeps) and keep it, this sun-dried tomato like a shrivelled heart, a broken *Oh*? The instruction manual for falling out of love says save the tomato, salt-sweet and crushed and tired, so tired.

Nothin' but a pain in your heart

It starts with nothin' then becomes a pain. A blue pain, dark. And the dog barks without knowin'. Your heart beats without livin'. Strange, this day you fall. Fallin' in love and everythin' in life should fall into place sweetly, softly. Fall out of love and that's somethin' you'll remember till your dyin' day. The woman sings her heart out. Then her soul. Everything around her disappears. The club is a long pause. Out of shadows and the dark, neon lights and her mouth. Out of her glittering voice, that something. Listen, backstage, with her gold lamé dress on the hanger, the woman's heart disappears. Then, her soul, crushing the empty. There's a knock on the door, a man says "I'll meet you downstairs." Everything in her life falls. Strange, this day, a dog howling. It starts with nothing, then becomes a pain. A blue, dark stain. A bruise from the falling.

Translation of a Misunderstanding

That time when I didn't smile and he said *Smile, then,* so it was my face talking or not talking[1], the body has language, and the face, too. *Strange girl*[2], he said, *but I love you.* Even that was a kind of misunderstanding because love goes both ways, smile or no smile, it takes two to tango. That time when my body misunderstood the steps – *You have no rhythm but I love you* – and we waltzed and I said *Let's stop, let's stop* and I was misunderstood and later in bed he said *Something's changed* and I said *No*[3], I meant *Yes,* said *Yes*[4], meant *No,* but in the morning I smiled and let him kiss me, *Strange girl but I love you.*

---

1. Those days of no smiles, when my face couldn't be translated by him.
2. Strange girl = I love you
3. No = Yes
4. Yes = No

Undoing my Hex

The witch bottle isn't big enough for what I want to put in it. Your shadow. Hair of the rug bought in a Tel Aviv market, it still tickles my heart. A snippet of a dream where we lie on grass, languishing, where Enter: your wife. Have you quite finished? she asks. I mix in some words from my mouth, half-words, because I'm mumbling. A pinch of salt, broken charcoal, incense, crisp blue egg-shells. A thimble-full of bottle-green sea water, a plucked peacock feather, the eyes of a dove. Anything to fill the emptiness. Anything racked from memory, the potion will make me retch. There's this rule that forbids you from calling an ex after-hours, it is bad manners. I offer the bottle *baksheesh*, a little tip, at the end. A smear of blood from the termination.

Uninhibited in Another Language

Not swear words but something I swear tastes of love
Watch your tongue watch your tongue romance Oh
With barbs I am modern when I speak Uninhibited
I am passionate and terrible My mother silent
dumbfounded thinks I've betrayed her slapped
her run off with that other language But no
I've returned I can say love you say love
tongue mother tongue and all the bad girl slang
Shall I spit it out spell it in bold beeps
or roll up my tongue till it hurts
My mouth fuck it has so much to say these days
On Sunday we go to church together

Hibiscus

Body my house / my horse my hound / what will I do / when you are fallen
— May Swenson

When I first touch my own body
it is want growing wild and soon my
fingers on slow-slow the wet soft house
petals and gasps and layers of electric oh my
where's my stallion oh god oh lovely horse
and sniffing at the lips of open bloom and my
pink sweet heat and now the hungry hound
of his bold mouth with the licking tongue and what
drips from it so loudly a trumpet so complete will
possess my voice which turns red purple and I
so smell the slippery blur of open close open do
more more with the crushed flower even when
I cry out even this bright colour of me on you
even when I and you are the sudden same are
blood drops soaking the final cry unpetalled fallen

The Singular of Paparazzi

My body is that orchid in the opening credits and Lady Gaga appears,
all sooty eyes and slutty gear. I love that her mouth recites filth in Swedish.
Then, the great fall. Lick these questions dipped in delicious poison:

How loud is anticlimax?
Did Minnie Mouse have black lips?
What is the singular of paparazzi?

[Police siren]
[Camera shutters]

She kills him and gets her own tea-cup, but I imagine
she still sheds tears sugary with I want, I want.

The Salesgirl says the Mannequin is Not for Sale

Marie Antoinette's shoes are cakes in pastel colours. She says she needs a friend, the salesgirl says they don't sell them here. She tries on a pair of flat shoes, her hair is flat, her heart is flat. Sparrows fly in and out of her bird-nest hair. She licks whipped cream off her fingers. The salesgirl brings more finger food. We need a splash of colour in the palace, says Marie Antoinette, I ordered hundreds of paints online: Sumptuous Plum, Cherry Glaze, Honey Drizzle, Pursuit of Happiness. Then she calls the palace: More shoe-shaped cakes, she mutters, though it sounds like an order. She turns to the salesgirl: I'd like to buy the mannequin. She's not for sale I'm afraid, says the salesgirl, who's been trained to say that, to whoever. I am not Whoever, cries Marie Antoinette. Her voice is torn. She takes shoes off the counter, bites them, spits out thread and buckles. One sparrow leaves her hair, bashes against the mirror and drops dead. Marie Antoinette picks it up, trembling with rage, starts plucking its feathers. The salesgirl dials 911. Let her eat cake, says the mannequin. Let her eat cake.

Millennium Bug

While you're all asleep and especially while you're asleep, I collect surnames from twenty years ago and put names to them or vice versa, and I turn the pages of yearbooks and that Bible with petal thin pages, thinking, how on earth did I get here, on this side of the planet, and I'm surprised that the answer is a bee buzzing in my heart, singing its monotonous stinging song, how on earth did it get there, I have no idea, but the night tells me we humans have this desperate need for Tomorrow and God, and God listens as we do that terrible countdown every night, and God says *To be honest I've lost count* and all I can think of is New Year's Eve 1999. The hotel ballroom was packed and we were swimming in champagne and vodka and that soprano boy sang. *I'm sorry* says the dream, *that's all we have time for.*

In which the Doctor speaks Gibberish

When he says tranquillizer of the triazolobenzodiazepine class,
he means Xanax, that planet inhabited by aliens.
Actually, she's been there, done that. He writes without looking up,
flicks through pages, finds her strange sky and asks Where do you fly?
She replies In cold places, in dull, grey-white happenings. Hesays
Are you so much better there than here? His mouth is blue, she notes.
He asks what her favourite moment was. So far, he adds.
The green wine, the green wine. And they have nothing more to say
except Think in and out, in and out, till she finally says
I'm doing my best to breathe.

The Great Wave

Sometimes I think of Hokusai. We're all drowning, and if there's God and even if there isn't, there's Hokusai and his wave. Inside the wave is a whale, inside the whale is a poem. None of us knows why this is happening. Hokusai is heading home on the night bus and there's a wave inside his head. Inside the wave is a wife, preparing dinner. She has no idea why her husband wallows in waves. There's always a wave, then another, and another, like history repeating itself. Inside history is a wave breaking, people waiting. Inside the waiting is an artist painting a wave each night, and inside the night are all his doubts, swelling. Sometimes I think of Hokusai and feel the weight of the wave inside my heart. Inside my heart is a lifeboat and inside the lifeboat is a poem. Hokusai and his wife drink green tea and inside the teacup is a wave. Inside the wave is a voice playing dead. Meanwhile, we're falling, we're falling, and none of us knows when the next wave is coming.

Feet in the Bowl

Let me wash your feet in milk.
Tell me how sweet and cooling it was
eighteen years later, when we meet again.
You are my daughter and do you see, do you know,
that the hardest part of love is keeping milk
from going sour? One day, they will tell you.

Let me hold you. Let me hold you again,
before the scene changes
and you run barefoot into other rooms.

Acknowledgements

Grateful acknowledgements to the following publications where some of these poems first appeared, sometimes in earlier versions: *Perverse 7, Mslexia, Anthropocene,* the *Live Canon 2022 Anthology, Footprints: an anthology of new ecopoetry, Sparks, Patchwork Lit Mag, SAND Journal, The Broken Spine Artist Collective, Streetcake Magazine, The Stony Thursday Book, Atrium, Poetry International, Raceme, Visual Verse, Ink Sweat &Tears, The Interpreter's House, Under Your Pillow.*

The poem *I have made a note of–* was commissioned by the Poetry Society/EUNIC and written as part of a collaboration with the poet Jacqueline Saphra in 2022.

Heartfelt thanks to Aaron Kent and Charlie Baylis for their professionalism and faith in my work.

Thanks are also due to all those who encouraged me along the road to publication: notably Pascale Petit, who selected *Iktsuarpok* as one of the finalists in the 2021 Mslexia Poetry Competition, and Helen Eastman and Jacqueline Saphra, who were a source of inspiration and kept me writing in difficult times.

My deepest gratitude to Richard Law for believing in me from the beginning. This collection would not have grown into its present form had it not been for his love, patience, unfailing support and invaluable editing. Richard, we make poetry together.

LAY OUT YOUR UNREST

Printed in the USA
CPSIA information can be obtained
at www.ICGtesting.com
CBHW030750201223
2790CB00005B/107